DISCLAIMER

This book is meant for
entertainment purposes only and
should not be viewed as a guide
for a marriage of any kind.

5:00 am
Wake up early to prepare for your husband's day.

5:05 am
Get yourself looking presentable,
so he is not frightened in the morning.

5:15 am

Pick out a pretty dress so he has something pleasant to look at.
Don't look frumpy!

5:20 am

Bring in the newspaper. Remove the sports section
and place on top of the newspaper for easy access.

5:25 am
Have the coffee ready. He works tirelessly
and should be rewarded with freshly ground brew.

5:30 am

Good wives will make sure their husband's have a home-cooked meal to begin the day. Anything less, could be seen as spousal abuse.

6:00 am
Once your husband is awake and has everything he needs,
run his car to the gas station and fill it up.

6:30 am
Iron any clothing your husband has laid out. If he changes
his mind about what to wear, continue ironing until he is satisfied.

7:00 am

Quietly chew gum, so you are not tempted to speak
and it helps maintain mouth strength and endurance.

8:00 am

Once your husband leaves, begin cutting the lawn. Be sure to cut diagonally in both directions. Your husband has standards.

8:00 am
Start his laundry. Follow his clothing labels wash instructions perfectly, especially the hand wash only items.

8:30 am
Your husband pays the electricity bill,
so hang the clothes on the line whenever possible.

9:00 am

Sweep, mop and dust thoroughly because your husband should not be exposed to potentially harmful dust particles.

10:00 am

Vacuum all furniture and carpets because you may have stirred up dust while sweeping.

11:45am
Use a knife to remove crusts, so he can enjoy his sandwich.
Make sure it is ready on the table when he gets home for lunch.

1:00 pm
Mend his clothes as needed. If time permits, make a
new dress for yourself from scrap material.

5:15 pm
Present him with a cold drink on a warm day. He needs a few hours to relax after working so hard.

5:30 pm

Allow him to rest his feet on the ottoman. If you do
not have an ottoman, you must become an ottoman.

6:00 pm
Have meat, potatoes and vegetables ready for him. Make sure there is also a variety of fresh baked desserts available.

6:30 pm
A good wife will have all dishes clean or out of sight.
Your husband should not be exposed to filthy dishes.

7:00 pm

Get a warm bucket of soapy water to hand wash your husband's car, while he rests after supper.

9:00 pm
He worked all day, now it is your turn to do all the work.
Your husband needs to feel your appreciation in your efforts.

10:00 pm

If you are up later than your husband, on your phone or watching TV, use earphones, so you don't interrupt his well earned rest.

There are so many benefits if you give your husband the love and environment he deserves. If you are a good enough wife, your husband may let you use the car to pick up groceries or even be considered worthy enough to carry his offspring. He will decide and tell you, when he is ready. Don't ask!

A life of service to your husband is a privilege.

Ladies, be proud to call yourselves wives, it is the best job a woman could ever have.